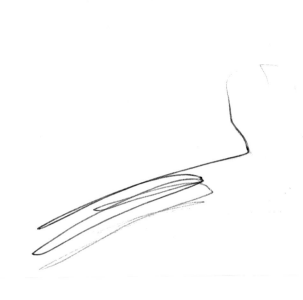

Spanish Words at School

By Sydney Salazar

Gareth Stevens
Publishing

Please visit our website, www.garethstevens.com. For a free color catalog of all our high-quality books, call toll free 1-800-542-2595 or fax 1-877-542-2596.

Library of Congress Cataloging-in-Publication Data

Salazar, Sydney.
Spanish words at school / by Sydney Salazar.
 p. cm. — (Learn my language! Spanish)
Includes index.
ISBN 978-1-4824-0338-1 (pbk.)
ISBN 978-1-4824-0340-4 (6-pack)
ISBN 978-1-4824-0334-3 (library binding)
1. Schools — Juvenile literature. 2. Vocabulary — Juvenile literature. 3. Spanish language — Vocabulary — Juvenile literature. I. Title.
PC4129.E5 S25 2014
468—dc23

First Edition

Published in 2014 by
Gareth Stevens Publishing
111 East 14th Street, Suite 349
New York, NY 10003

Copyright © 2014 Gareth Stevens Publishing

Designer: Sarah Liddell
Editor: Therese Shea

Photo credits: Cover, p. 1 Africa Studio/Shutterstock.com; p. 5 Andy Dean Photography/Shutterstock.com; p. 7 Christopher Futcher/the Agency Collection/Getty Images; p. 9 Darrin Henry/Shutterstock.com; p. 11 Ambient Ideas/Shutterstock.com; p. 13 michaeljung/Shutterstock.com; p. 15 © iStockphoto.com/PacoRomero; p. 17 oliveromg/Shutterstock.com; p. 19 Jaimie Duplass/Shutterstock.com; p. 21 iStockphoto.com/kali9.

Printed in the United States of America

CPSIA compliance information: Batch #CW14GS: For further information contact Gareth Stevens, New York, New York at 1-800-542-2595.

Contents

Boldface words appear in the glossary.

Español at School

Do you speak *español*? That's the Spanish word for Spanish! School is a great place to start. The Spanish word for school is *escuela*. Look in the box on each page to learn how to say the Spanish words.

school = escuela (ehs-KWAY-lah)

Spanish = español (ehs-pah-NYOHL)

escuela

5

My Teacher

This is my teacher. He likes to tell jokes. He's very funny! The Spanish word for male teacher is *maestro*. The Spanish word for female teacher is *maestra*.

male teacher = maestro (mah-EHS-troh)

female teacher = maestra (mah-EHS-trah)

English Class

The Spanish word for class is *clase*. My *clase* writes **poems** at our desks. *Escritorio* is Spanish for desk. How many people are in your *clase*?

class = clase (KLAH-seh)

desk = escritorio (ehs-Kree-TOH-ryoh)

escritorio

9

Math Class

It's word problem day in math class. The Spanish word for pencil is *lápiz*. The Spanish word for paper is *papel*. I **solve** a tricky math problem with my *lápiz* and *papel*!

pencil = lápiz (LAH-peez)

paper = papel (pah-PEHL)

lápiz

papel

11

Gym

Let's head to gym class. Today, the class plays soccer. The Spanish word for soccer is *fútbol*. *Pelota* is the word for ball. Can you kick the *pelota* and score a goal?

soccer = fútbol (FOOT-bohl)

ball = pelota (peh-LOH-tah)

pelota

13

Lunch

Are you hungry? It's time to eat lunch. *Comer* means "to eat" in Spanish. Let's have soup today. The Spanish word for soup is *sopa*. I love chicken *sopa*! Yum!

to eat = comer (koh-MEHR)

soup = sopa (SOH-pah)

sopa

15

Science Class

It's time for **science** class! The Spanish word for science is *ciencia*. We're doing an **experiment** with plants. *Planta* is Spanish for plant. My *planta* was the tallest!

science = ciencia (SYEN-syah)

plant = planta (PLAHN-tah)

planta

17

School Library

It's time to go to the school library! The Spanish word for library is *biblioteca*. We each check out a book, or *libro*. Do you want a *libro* to take home?

library = biblioteca (bee-blyoh-TEH-kah)

book = libro (LEE-broh)

libro

19

Adiós

It's time to go home! We say *adiós*, or goodbye, to our friends. We also say, *"Hasta mañana."* That means "see you tomorrow."

goodbye = adiós (ah-DYOHS)

see you tomorrow = hasta mañana
(AHS-tah mah-NYAH-nah)

Glossary

experiment: a test to figure out if something will happen

poem: a piece of writing that has lines of a certain length and sometimes tells a story

science: the study of the world around us

solve: to find the answer

For More Information

Books

Lawless, Laura K. *The Everything Kids' Learning Spanish Book*. Avon, MA: Adams Media, 2006.

Marsh, Carole. *"Way to Go, Amigo!" English for Kids*. Peachtree City, GA: Gallopade International, 2007.

Wightwick, Jane. *Way-Cool Spanish Phrase Book*. New York, NY: McGraw-Hill, 2005.

Websites

Spanish for Kids
www.123teachme.com/learn_spanish/spanish_for_children
Learn how to say colors, numbers, and more in Spanish.

Spanish—School Day
www.bbc.co.uk/schools/primarylanguages/spanish/school_day/
Practice school-related Spanish words and phrases.

Index